A Workbook for Fundamentals of Speech

Ann J. Atkinson, Ph.D.

Keene State College

KENDALL/HUNT PUBLISHING COMPANY
4050 Westmark Drive   Dubuque, Iowa 52002

Cover image © 2004 PhotoDisc, Inc.

ISBN 0-7575-1464-2

Printed in the United States of America
10 9 8 7 6 5 4 3 2 1

Table of Contents

Round III—Speech to Persuade

Introduction

A Workbook for Fundamentals of Speech is designed to provide you with many of the handouts that you will need to use as you prepare practice speeches and then plan, deliver, and evaluate your own speeches during the semester. You will need to bring the workbook with you to each class meeting since time will be spent explaining the materials and some of the work sheets will be used for group and individual exercises during class time.

The materials will assist you with the planning and performance of four speeches--the narrative speech, two speeches to inform, and the speech to persuade. For each of these speeches, you will practice planning as a member of a group, and then prepare a formal outline and create multiple introductions and conclusions for your speech. You will then choose the introduction and the conclusion that you view to be the best ones for the actual speech. Work sheets for the preparation of the key word outline--the outline you will develop for rehearsal and then use during the performance of each speech--are also included.

You will provide your instructor with evaluation sheets for your formal outline and for your performance, evaluate your peers, and evaluate your own performance. The instructor evaluation sheets include the numbers of points that are allotted for each of the outlines, research materials, and for your performances. This workbook has been prepared for use in all sections of COMM 171—*Fundamentals of Speech*. Your instructor may wish to alter these stated point values. If so, your instructor will explain the adjustments as you begin planning each of the speeches. The stated point system allots 550 points of 1000 points to the preparation and delivery of the four speeches. The remaining 450 points would be used for quizzes and a final examination and for rewarding class participation.

You have several roles to play as a student in this course. As a speaker, you are responsible to plan, perform, and evaluate your speeches. As a member of the audience, you are responsible to critique the speeches of your peers. You will improve as a public speaker as you react to your instructor's critique, to your self-critique, and to the messages delivered by the other students in the class.

The workbook is intended to supplement the material in your textbook, *The Challenge of Effective Speaking*, 12th edition, by Rudolph F. Verderber and Kathleen S. Verderber and the material covered in the lectures delivered by your instructor.

When you have finished using the materials in the workbook, you will be asked to evaluate their usefulness to you. With the workbook's institution as a required text for COMM 171—*Fundamentals of Speech*, we have labored to provide you with meaningful exercises for understanding and demonstrating facility with communication concepts. We have also attempted to assist you with the preparation of outlines and bibliographies. Finally, the workbook serves to standardize the course requirements and the evaluation procedures across the many sections of COMM 171—*Fundamentals of Speech* that are offered each semester. We want you to help us to accomplish these critically important goals by sharing your assessment of the workbook with us.

Ann J. Atkinson
Keene, New Hampshire
July 2004

Student Questionnaire

Name_____

Hometown_____Class Year_____

Current/Campus Address_____

_____

Current/Campus Phone_____E-mail_____

Program of Study/Major_____

Please respond briefly to the following questions, using a pen. Return completed questionnaire to your instructor.

1. You are at a job interview. Your interviewer tells you the job you're applying for will involve a lot of public speaking. What thought flashes through your mind?

2. Name a national political or public figure who you believe is a good speaker, and briefly discuss why.

3. Are you involved in any extracurricular activities? If you are, please list them.

4. What work of fiction have you read most recently?

5. List two or three authors whose work you admire.

6. List one or two television shows you enjoy watching.

7. Which news program do you view for the nightly news?

8. Of the films you've seen in the last year, name a couple that you especially enjoyed.

9. Do you have any hobbies? If yes, please list them.

10. Do you participate in recreational sports (tennis, golf, racquetball, bicycling, etc.)? If yes, please list them.

11. When did you give your last speech? What was the topic? Were you pleased with your performance? Explain.

12. What would you like to be doing in ten years?

Work Sheet for Narrative Speech Assignment

Instructions: Research the day you were born. What was going on in the world? Consider discovering the following:

- the headlines of newspapers such as the *Boston Globe* and the *New York Times*
- cover stories for newsmagazines such as *Time* and *Newsweek*
- titles of popular songs and names of popular music artists
- names of popular films and film stars
- names of popular books and authors
- discussions of important political issues of the day
- important speeches on the issues
- discussions of important social issues of the day
- comments or speeches by experts
- discussions of scientific discoveries
- comments or speeches by experts
- discussions of important issues in the specific place where you were born

Consult at least five (5) sources (to include but not limited to newspapers, newsmagazines, almanacs). Then craft a speech of introduction that is one to two (1-2) minutes in length. The speech must have a recognizable introduction (attention-getter and preview), body, and conclusion (summary and emphasis), with appropriate transitions. Turn in a typed outline of your speech, along with a bibliography of your sources, in APA style.

Due Date:_____

Format for Typed Outline for Narrative Speech

Introduction:

Attention-getter:

Preview (main points of the body of the speech):

Transition (phrase or statement which serves as a bridge or a signpost):

Body:

I.

Transition:

II.

Transition:

III.

Transition:

Conclusion:

Summary (restatement of main points of the body of the speech):

Emphasis:

Bibliography (use APA style):

Work Sheet for Preparing Introduction and Conclusion for Narrative Speech

Introduction

      The introduction is composed of two parts: the attention-getter and the preview. You have a variety of choices to make as you consider your opening: (1) startling statement, (2) rhetorical question, (3) story, (4) personal reference, (5) quotation, and (6) suspense. Refer to chapter 8 of your textbook for detailed explanations of each type. Then choose three (3) of the six (6) types and write three (3) possible attention-getters for your speech.

1. Startling Statement:

2. Rhetorical Question:

3. Story:

4. Personal Reference:

5. Quotation:

6. Suspense:

Conclusion

The conclusion is composed of two parts: the summary and the statement of emphasis. In the statement of emphasis, you want to leave your audience with a lasting impression. You may achieve this goal by (1) telling a story, (2) using a quotation, (3) offering an example, or (4) making a startling statement. Select two (2) of the four (4) types, and write two (2) possible conclusions for your narrative speech.

1. Story:

2. Quotation:

3. Example:

4. Startling Statement:

Work Sheet for Preparing the Key Word Outline for Narrative Speech

All of your speeches for this course will be delivered extemporaneously, which means that each speech will be prepared and practiced, then delivered to an audience using a conversational tone and establishing nearly continuous eye contact. To that end, you will prepare detailed outlines during the preparation phase, and key word outlines for use during the rehearsal stage and during the performance of the speech.

For the Narrative Speech, you will use one 4"x 6" card and turn it in to your instructor following your performance of the speech. Write the Attention-Getter and the Statement of Emphasis in full. Use key words or short phrases that will remind you of your transitions and the main points of the Body of the speech.

Attention-Getter: Write in full.

Preview: Main points of the body of the speech.

Transition:

I.

Transition:

II.

Transition:

III.

Transition:

Summary: Main points of the body of the speech.

Emphasis: Write in full.

Criteria Used for Evaluating Student Speeches in Fundamentals of Speech
Adapted from criteria established by the National Communication Association

The average speech (the "C" speech) should meet the following criteria:
1. Conform to the kind of speech assigned (informative, persuasive).
2. Be ready for presentation on the assigned date.
3. Conform to the time limit.
4. Fulfill any special requirements of the assignment, such as contacting professor via E-mail during the preparation phase of the speech, preparing and submitting a typed outline the class day before the performance, using visual aids.
5. Have a clear specific purpose and central idea.
6. Have an identifiable introduction, body, and conclusion.
7. Cite sources for all supporting materials.
8. Show reasonable directness and competence in delivery.

The above-average speech (the "B" speech) should meet the preceding criteria and ALSO:
1. Deal with a challenging topic.
2. Fulfill all major functions of a speech introduction and conclusion.
3. Display clear organization of main points and supporting details.
4. Support main points with evidence that meets the tests of accuracy, relevance, objectivity, and sufficiency.
5. Exhibit proficient use of connectives: transitions, internal previews, internal summaries.
6. Be delivered skillfully enough so as not to distract attention from the speaker's message.

The superior speech (the "A" speech) should meet all the preceding criteria and ALSO:
1. Constitute a genuine contribution by the speaker to the knowledge or beliefs of the audience.
2. Sustain positive interest, feeling, and/or commitment among the audience.
3. Contain elements of vividness and special interest in the use of language.
4. Be delivered in a fluent, polished manner that strengthens the impact of the speaker's message.

The below-average speech (the "D" speech) does not meet one or more of the standards of a "C" speech and:
1. Is obviously unrehearsed.
2. Is based upon biased information or unsupported opinions.

A failing speech (the "F" speech) does not meet three or more of the standards of a "C" speech, reflects either of the problems associated with a "D" speech, or:
1. Uses fabricated supporting materials.
2. Deliberately distorts evidence.
3. Is plagiarized.

Work Sheet for Preparing the Practice Speech to Inform Prior to Round I

Group's Assignment: Prepare a speech of five to seven (5-7) minutes to inform with the use of visual aids. Because you will be completing the assignment during class time, the speech will be a work in progress. The assignment is designed to help you to use your textbook as a resource while selecting a topic, and researching and organizing a speech. Before you begin preparing the speech, select a group member who will act as the spokesperson for your group when your group is called upon to share your efforts with the class.

Planning Phase
Topic:

Specific Goal (phrased in terms of the audience):

Thesis Statement (three main points):

Method of Organization (chronological or topical):

Presentation
Introduction, divided into two sections:
    Attention-Getter:
    Preview:

Transition (phrase or statement that serves as a bridge or a signpost):

Body:

I.
    A.

        1.
        2.

    B.
        1.
        2.

Transition:

II.

    A.

        1.

        2.

    B.

        1.

        2.

Transition:

III.

    A.

        1.

        2.

    B.

        1.

        2.

Transition:

Conclusion, divided into two sections:
    Summary:
    Emphasis:

Work Sheet for Preparing Typed Outline for Round I—Speech to Inform

Assignment: Prepare a speech of five to seven (5-7) minutes to inform with the use of visual aids. You must cite three (3) sources in the body of the speech and include a bibliography of five (5) sources with your typed outline. Citations for quoted or paraphrased materials must include the following information: (1) who is writing (or speaking), (2) when the information was collected or reported, and (3) where the information appears.

Sources to consider include full-length works, magazine articles, journal articles, newspaper articles, and televised documentaries. Interviews with experts in your topic area may also be used as source material. You must include a photocopy of the first page of three (3) of your five (5) sources with your typed outline and bibliography. Use complete sentences in the outline.

Due Date: _2/7/05_

Planning Phase

Topic:
Volleyball

Specific Goal:
To inform about the sport of Volleyball

Thesis Statement:
To share with the audience my personal experience with the sport, and to talk about my passion for volleyball.

Method of Organization (topical, chronological, or causal):
Topical

Presentation

Introduction, divided into two sections:
    Attention-getter:
    Preview:

Transition:

Body:

I.
    A.
        1.
        2.

    B.
        1.
        2.

Citation (who, where, and when):

Transition:

II.

    A.
        1.
        2.

    B.
        1.
        2.

Citation (who, where, and when):

Transition:

III.

    A.
        1.
        2.

    B.
        1.
        2.

Citation (who, where, and when):

Transition:

Conclusion, divided into two sections:
    Summary:
    Emphasis:

Bibliography (use APA style):

Work Sheet for Preparing Introduction and Conclusion for
Round I—Speech to Inform

Introduction
      The introduction is composed of two parts: the attention-getter and the preview. You have a variety of choices to make as you consider your opening: (1) startling statement, (2) rhetorical question, (3) story, (4) personal reference, (5) quotation, and (6) suspense. Refer to chapter 8 of your textbook for detailed explanations of each type. Then choose three (3) of the six (6) types and write three (3) possible attention-getters for your speech.

1. Startling Statement:

2. Rhetorical Question:

3. Story:

4. Personal Reference:

5. Quotation:

6. Suspense:

Conclusion

The conclusion is composed of two parts: the summary and the statement of emphasis. In the statement of emphasis, you want to leave your audience with a lasting impression. You may achieve this goal by (1) telling a story, (2) using a quotation, (3) offering an example, or (4) making a startling statement. Select two (2) of the four (4) types, and write two (2) possible conclusions for your speech to inform.

1. Story:

2. Quotation:

3. Example:

4. Startling Statement:

Work Sheet about Use of APA Style

All of your speeches include conducting research and producing a bibliography in APA style. Let's say you are considering a speech to inform about the myths associated with becoming fit. You know that Gina Kolata, science reporter for the *New York Times*, has written a book about fitness, so you decide to begin there. You search *Keene-Link* and find that Mason Library holds the book. Then you consult *Academic Search Premier at EBSCOhost* to see what has been written in general and specialty magazines. What follows is a bibliography of five (5) sources in APA style about the myths associated with becoming fit. The sources are divided by type and then placed in alphabetical order.

A Book by One Author:
Author. (Year of Publication). *Title*. Place of Publication: Publisher.

Kolata, G. (2003). *Ultimate fitness: The quest for truth about exercise and health*. New York:

   Farrar, Straus and Giroux.

An Article in a Monthly Magazine:
Author. (Year, Month of issue). Article title. *Magazine Title, volume number,* page numbers.

Quill, S., & Avedon, G. (2004, June). 7 muscle myths. *Men's Health, 19,* 130-132.

Tecco, B.D. (2004, March). Fitness myths exposed! *Current Health, 30,* 30-31.

An Article in a Monthly Magazine—No Author Given:
Article title. (Year, Month of issue). *Magazine Title, volume number,* page numbers.

Experts debunk weight loss myths. (2003, September). *Environmental Nutrition, 26,* 3.

An Article in a Newspaper:
Author. (Year, Date of issue). Article title. *Name of Newspaper,* page abbreviation. Sectionpage. (Note: No punctuation or space between section letter, capped, and page number.)

Zimmer, J. (1996, October 9). New in aerobics: Pumping rope. *New York Times,* p. C1.

On the reverse side of this page is the completed reference list as it should be presented with your typed outline for each speech.

References

Experts debunk weight loss myths. (2003, September). *Environmental Nutrition, 26,* 3.

Kolata, G. (2003). *Ultimate fitness: The quest for truth about exercise and health.* New York:

Farrar, Straus and Giroux.

Quill, S., & Avedon, G. (2004, June). 7 muscle myths. *Men's Health, 19,* 130-132.

Tecco, B.D. (2004, March). Fitness myths exposed! *Current Health, 30,* 30-31.

Zimmer, J. (1996, October 9). New in aerobics: Pumping rope. *New York Times,* p. C1.

Work Sheet for Preparing Key Word Outline for Round I—Speech to Inform

All of your speeches for this course will be delivered extemporaneously, which means each speech will be prepared, practiced, and delivered to an audience using a conversational tone and establishing nearly continuous eye contact. To that end, you will prepare detailed outlines during the preparation phase, and key word outlines for use during the rehearsal stage and during the performance of the speech.

For the Speech to Inform, you will use two 4"x 6" cards and turn them in to your instructor following your performance of the speech. Card #1: Write the Attention-Getter and the Statement of Emphasis in full. Use key words or short phrases that will remind you of your transitions and the main points of the Body of the speech. Insert indicators of the placement of the citations (C1, C2, C3). Card #2: Include the material you will cite--statistics, testimonials, and examples--and who is writing, where, and when.

Card #1:
Attention-Getter: Write in full.
Preview: Main points of the body of the speech.
Transition:
I.
C1
Transition:
II.
C2
Transition:
III.
C3
Transition:
Summary: Main points of the body of the speech.
Emphasis: Write in full.

Card #2:
Statistics, testimonials, and examples, with who is writing, where, and when.
Citation #1:

Citation #2:

Citation #3:

Instructor's Checklist for Typed Outline for Round I—Speech to Inform

On the day you turn in your typed outline for this round of speeches, provide your instructor with this checklist. It will be used to grade your outline. Points: ____/60

Specific Goal (2):
____Specific goal is not included.
____Specific goal is not worded in terms of the audience.

Thesis Statement (3):
____Thesis statement is not included.
____Thesis statement does not include the three (3) main points of the body of the speech.

Method of Organization (3):
____Method of organization is not noted.
____Method of organization is incorrectly noted.

Introduction (6):
____Introduction is not included in the outline.
____Introduction does not include an attention-getter.
____Introduction does not include a preview.
____Preview does not include the three (3) main points of the body of the speech.

Transitions (8):
____Transitions are not included in the outline. ___#1 ___#2 ___#3 ___#4
____Transitions do not serve as signposts or bridges to the next section of the speech.
                               ___#1 ___#2 ___#3 ___#4

Body (9):
____Outline of the body of the speech is not sufficiently detailed.
____Complete sentences are not used.
____Complete sentences are not used throughout the outline.
____Incorrect format is used.

Citations (9):
____Citations are not included in the outline. ___#1 ___#2 ___#3
____Citations are incomplete. ___#1 ___#2 ___#3

Conclusion (6):
____Conclusion is not included in the outline.
____Conclusion does not include a summary.
____Summary does not include the three (3) main points of the body of the speech.
____Conclusion does not include a statement of emphasis.

Bibliography (14):

_____Five (5) sources are not included.

_____Incorrect format is used. APA style is required.

_____Photocopies of first page of three (3) of five (5) sources are not included.

Instructor's Evaluation Form for Round I—Speech to Inform

Before you go to the front of the classroom to deliver your speech, provide your instructor with this form. It will be used to grade your performance.

Speaker:_____ Date:_____

Time: _____

Rating Scale:	Excellent	Good	Average	Fair	Poor
	5	4	3	2	1

INTRODUCTION:____
 Gains attention
 Reveals the topic clearly
 Relates topic to the audience
 Establishes credibility
 Previews the body of the speech
Comments:_____

_____

BODY: ____
 Main points clear
 Main points fully supported
 Citations complete
 Organization well planned
 Language accurate
 Language clear
 Language appropriate
 Transitions effective
Comments:_____

_____

CONCLUSION: ____
 Prepares audience for ending
 Reinforces the central idea
 Ends on a strong note
Comments:_____

_____

DELIVERY: ____
  Begins without rushing
  Maintains strong eye contact
  Avoids distracting mannerisms
  Articulates words clearly
  Uses pauses effectively
  Uses vocal variety to add impact
  Communicates enthusiasm
  Presents visual aids well
  Departs from the lectern without rushing
Comments:_____

_____

OVERALL EVALUATION____
Comments:_____

_____

_____

Maximum Points: 150   Points for Speech:_____/90 + Outline:_____/60

Total Points for Round:_____   Letter Grade:_____

Speech /90	Speech + Outline /150
A = 85.5	A = 142.5-150
AB = 81	AB = 135.0-142.4
B = 76.5	B = 127.5-134.9
BC = 72	BC = 120.0-127.4
C = 67.5	C = 112.5-119.9
CD = 63	CD = 105.0-112.4
D = 58.5	D = 97.5-104.9
F = Below 54	F = Below 90

Self-Evaluation of Performance of Speech to Inform—Round I

Name_____

Date_____

Due: Class day after you perform your speech. Please record your responses to the questions in pen.

What were the best aspects of your speech? Give specific examples.
Organization:
  Method:

  Proportion:

  Wording:

  Delivery:

What, if anything, would you like to change about your speech?
Planning:

Organization:
  Method:

  Proportion:

Wording:

Delivery:

Estimate the number of hours you spent selecting your topic, researching the topic, and organizing the speech. Selecting topic_____ Researching speech_____ Organizing speech_____

Estimate the number of hours you spent rehearsing the speech. _____
What strategies did you use as you rehearsed the speech (rehearsed in front of friends, rehearsed in front of a mirror, rehearsed with a timer, rehearsed with a key word outline)?

How would you characterize your performance of this speech (outstanding, good, average, below average or poor) and why? Refer to the sheet called "Criteria Used for Evaluating Student Speeches in Fundamentals of Speech" in this workbook as you answer this question.

Peer Evaluation Form for Round I—Speech to Inform

Speaker:_____ Date:_____

Topic: _____ Time:_____ Critiquer: _____

Rating Scale:	Excellent	Good	Average	Fair	Poor
	5	4	3	2	1

Introduction: ____
  Gains attention
  Reveals the topic clearly
  Relates topic to the audience
  Establishes credibility
  Previews the body of the speech
Comments:_____

_____

Body: List the main points of the speech. On the line at right, note the kinds of supporting materials the speaker uses for each: (S) statistics; (E) examples; (T) testimonials.

Main Point   Supporting Materials

I._____   _____

II._____   _____

III._____   _____

Do the citations include the following information: who, where, and when?

  Citation #1_____

  Citation #2_____

  Citation #3_____

What pattern of organization does the speaker use for the body of the speech? (topical, chronological, or causal order)_____

	Excellent	Good	Average	Fair	Poor
	5	4	3	2	1

Conclusion: ____
  Reinforces the central idea
  Ends on a strong note

	Excellent 5	Good 4	Average 3	Fair 2	Poor 1
Delivery: ____					
Speaker's language clear					
Speaker's language appropriate					
Speaker maintains strong eye contact					
Speaker articulates words clearly					
Speaker seems poised and confident					
Speaker communicates enthusiasm					

Overall evaluation of speech:_____

_____

Peer Evaluation Form for Round I—Speech to Inform

Speaker:_____ Date:_____

Topic: _____ Time:_____ Critiquer: _____

Rating Scale:	Excellent	Good	Average	Fair	Poor
	5	4	3	2	1

Introduction: ____
  Gains attention
  Reveals the topic clearly
  Relates topic to the audience
  Establishes credibility
  Previews the body of the speech
Comments:_____

_____

Body: List the main points of the speech. On the line at right, note the kinds of supporting materials the speaker uses for each: (S) statistics; (E) examples; (T) testimonials.

Main Point   Supporting Materials

I._____   _____

II._____   _____

III._____   _____

Do the citations include the following information: who, where, and when?

     Citation #1_____

     Citation #2_____

     Citation #3_____

What pattern of organization does the speaker use for the body of the speech? (topical, chronological, or causal order)_____

	Excellent	Good	Average	Fair	Poor
	5	4	3	2	1

Conclusion: ____
  Reinforces the central idea
  Ends on a strong note

	Excellent	Good	Average	Fair	Poor
	5	4	3	2	1

Delivery: ____
    Speaker's language clear
    Speaker's language appropriate
    Speaker maintains strong eye contact
    Speaker articulates words clearly
    Speaker seems poised and confident
    Speaker communicates enthusiasm

Overall evaluation of speech:_____

_____

Peer Evaluation Form for Round I—Speech to Inform

Speaker:_____ Date:_____

Topic: _____ Time:_____Critiquer: _____

Rating Scale:	Excellent	Good	Average	Fair	Poor
	5	4	3	2	1

Introduction: ____
  Gains attention
  Reveals the topic clearly
  Relates topic to the audience
  Establishes credibility
  Previews the body of the speech
Comments:_____

_____

Body: List the main points of the speech. On the line at right, note the kinds of supporting materials the speaker uses for each: (S) statistics; (E) examples; (T) testimonials.

Main Point   Supporting Materials

I._____   _____

II._____   _____

III._____   _____

Do the citations include the following information: who, where, and when?

   Citation #1_____

   Citation #2_____

   Citation #3_____

What pattern of organization does the speaker use for the body of the speech? (topical, chronological, or causal order)_____

	Excellent	Good	Average	Fair	Poor
	5	4	3	2	1

Conclusion: ____
  Reinforces the central idea
  Ends on a strong note

	Excellent 5	Good 4	Average 3	Fair 2	Poor 1

Delivery: ____
  Speaker's language clear
  Speaker's language appropriate
  Speaker maintains strong eye contact
  Speaker articulates words clearly
  Speaker seems poised and confident
  Speaker communicates enthusiasm

Overall evaluation of speech:_____

_____

Work Sheet for Preparing the Practice Speech to Inform Prior to Round II

Group's Assignment: Prepare a speech of five to seven (5-7) minutes to inform with the use of visual aids. Because you will be completing the assignment during class time, the speech will be a work in progress. The assignment is designed to help you to use your textbook as a resource while selecting a topic, and researching and organizing a speech. Before you begin preparing the speech, select a group member who will act as the spokesperson for your group when your group is called upon to share your efforts with the class.

Planning Phase
Topic:

Specific Goal (phrased in terms of the audience):

Thesis Statement (three main points):

Method of Organization (chronological or topical):

Presentation
Introduction, divided into two sections:
    Attention-Getter:
    Preview:

Transition (phrase or statement that serves as a bridge or a signpost):

Body:

I.
    A.

        1.
        2.

    B.
        1.
        2.

Transition:

II.

    A.
        1.
        2.

    B.
        1.
        2.

Transition:

III.

    A.
        1.
        2.

    B.
        1.
        2.

Transition:

Conclusion, divided into two sections:
    Summary:
    Emphasis:

Work Sheet for Preparing Typed Outline for Round II—Speech to Inform

Assignment: Prepare a speech of five to seven (5-7) minutes to inform with the use of visual aids. You must cite three (3) sources in the body of the speech and include a bibliography of five (5) sources with your typed outline. Citations for quoted or paraphrased materials must include the following information: who is writing (or speaking), when the information has been collected or reported, and where the information appears.

Sources to consider include full-length works, magazine articles, journal articles, newspaper articles, and televised documentaries. Interviews with experts in your topic area may also be used as source material. You must include a photocopy of the first page of three (3) of your five (5) sources with your typed outline and bibliography, which is due the class day before you deliver your speech. Use complete sentences in the outline.

Due Date:_____

Planning Phase
Topic:

Specific Goal:

Thesis Statement:

Method of Organization:

Presentation
Introduction, divided into two sections:
      Attention-Getter:
      Preview:

Transition:

Body:

I.
    A.
        1.
        2.

    B.
        1.
        2.

Citation (who, where, and when):

Transition:

II.

    A.
        1.
        2.

    B.
        1.
        2.

Citation (who, where, and when):

Transition:

III.

    A.
        1.
        2.

    B.
        1.
        2.

Citation (who, where, and when):

Transition:

Conclusion, divided into two sections:
    Summary:
    Emphasis:

Bibliography (use APA style):

Work Sheet for Preparing Introduction and Conclusion for
Round II—Speech to Inform

Introduction

      The introduction is composed of two parts: the attention-getter and the preview. You have a variety of choices to make as you consider your opening: (1) startling statement, (2) rhetorical question, (3) story, (4) personal reference, (4) quotation, and (5) suspense. Refer to chapter 8 of your textbook for detailed explanations of each type. Then choose three (3) of the six (6) types and write three (3) possible attention-getters for your speech.

1. Startling Statement:

2. Rhetorical Question:

3. Story:

4. Personal Reference:

5. Quotation:

6. Suspense:

Conclusion

The conclusion is composed of two parts: the summary and the statement of emphasis. In the statement of emphasis, you want to leave your audience with a lasting impression. You may achieve this goal by (1) telling a story, (2) using a quotation, (3) offering an example, or (4) making a startling statement. Select two (2) of the four (4) types, and write two (2) possible conclusions for your speech to inform.

1. Story:

2. Quotation:

3. Example:

4. Startling Statement:

Work Sheet for Preparing Key Word Outline for Round II
Speech to Inform

All of your speeches for this course will be delivered extemporaneously, which means that each speech will be prepared, practiced, and delivered to an audience using a conversational tone and establishing nearly continuous eye contact. To that end, you will prepare detailed outlines during the preparation phase and key word outlines for use during the rehearsal stage and during the performance of the speech.

For the Speech to Inform, you will use two 4"x 6" cards and turn them in to your instructor following your performance of the speech. Card #1: Write the Attention-Getter and the Statement of Emphasis in full. Use key words or short phrases that will remind you of your transitions and the main points of the Body of the speech. Insert indicators of the placement of the citations (C1, C2, C3). Card #2: Include the material you will cite--statistics, testimonials, and examples--and who is writing, where, and when.

Card #1:
Attention-Getter: Write in full.
Preview: Main points of the body of the speech.
Transition:
I.
C1
Transition:
II.
C2
Transition:
III.
C3
Transition:
Summary: Main points of the body of the speech.
Emphasis: Write in full.

Card #2:
Statistics, testimonials, and examples, with who is writing, where and when.
Citation #1:

Citation #2:

Citation #3:

Instructor's Checklist for Typed Outline for Round II—Speech to Inform

On the day you turn in your typed outline for this round of speeches, provide your instructor with this checklist. It will be used to grade your outline. Points: _____/80

Specific Goal (4):
_____Specific goal is not included.
_____Specific goal is not worded in terms of the audience.

Thesis Statement (6):
_____Thesis statement is not included.
_____Thesis statement does not include the three (3) main points of the body of the speech.

Method of Organization (3):
_____Method of organization is not noted.
_____Method of organization is incorrectly noted.

Introduction (6):
_____Introduction is not included in the outline.
_____Introduction does not include an attention-getter.
_____Introduction does not include a preview.
_____Preview does not include the three (3) main points of the body of the speech.

Transitions (8):
_____Transitions are not included in the outline. ___#1 ___#2 ___#3 ___#4
_____Transitions do not serve as signposts or bridges to the next section of the speech.
                                             ___#1 ___#2 ___#3 ___#4

Body (18):
_____Outline of the body of the speech is not sufficiently detailed.
_____Complete sentences are not used.
_____Complete sentences are not used throughout the outline.
_____Incorrect format is used.

Citations (9):
_____Citations are not included in the outline. ___#1 ___#2 ___#3
_____Citations are incomplete. ___#1 ___#2 ___#3

Conclusion (6):
_____Conclusion is not included in the outline.
_____Conclusion does not include a summary.
_____Summary does not include the three (3) main points of the body of the speech.
_____Conclusion does not include a statement of emphasis.

Bibliography (20):

_____Five (5) sources are not included.

_____Incorrect format is used. APA style is required.

_____Photocopies of first page of three (3) of five (5) sources are not included.

Instructor's Evaluation Form for Round II—Speech to Inform

Before you go to the front of the classroom to deliver your speech, provide your instructor with this form. It will be used to grade your performance.

Speaker:_____ Date:_____

Time: _____

Rating Scale:	Excellent 5	Good 4	Average 3	Fair 2	Poor 1

INTRODUCTION:____
 Gains attention
 Reveals the topic clearly
 Relates topic to the audience
 Establishes credibility
 Previews the body of the speech
Comments:_____

_____

BODY: ____
 Main points clear
 Main points fully supported
 Citations complete
 Organization well planned
 Language accurate
 Language clear
 Language appropriate
 Transitions effective
Comments: _____

_____

CONCLUSION: ____
 Prepares audience for ending
 Reinforces the central idea
 Ends on a strong note
Comments: _____

_____

DELIVERY: ____
  Begins without rushing
  Maintains strong eye contact
  Avoids distracting mannerisms
  Articulates words clearly
  Uses pauses effectively
  Uses vocal variety to add impact
  Communicates enthusiasm
  Presents visual aids well
  Departs from the lectern without rushing
Comments:_____

_____

OVERALL EVALUATION____
Comments:_____

_____

_____

Maximum Points: 180   Points for Speech:_____/100 + Outline:_____/80

Total Points for Round:_____   Letter Grade:_____

Speech /100   Speech + Outline /180
A   = 95   A   = 171-180
AB = 90   AB = 162-170
B   = 85   B   = 153-161
BC = 80   BC = 144-152
C   = 75   C   = 135-143
CD = 70   CD = 126-134
D   = 65   D   = 117-125
F   = Below 60   F   = Below 108

Self-Evaluation of Performance of Speech to Inform—Round II

Name_____

Date_____

Due: Class day after you perform your speech. Please record your responses to the questions in pen.

What were the best aspects of your speech? Give specific examples.
Organization:
  Method:

  Proportion:

Wording:

Delivery:

What, if anything, would you like to change about your speech?
Planning:

Organization:
  Method:

  Proportion:

Wording:

Delivery:

Estimate the number of hours you spent selecting your topic, researching the topic, and organizing the speech. Selecting topic_____ Researching speech_____ Organizing speech_____

Estimate the number of hours you spent rehearsing the speech. _____
What strategies did you use as you rehearsed the speech (rehearsed in front of friends, rehearsed in front of a mirror, rehearsed with a timer, rehearsed with a key word outline)?

How would you characterize your performance of this speech (outstanding, good, average, below average or poor) and why? Refer to the sheet called "Criteria Used for Evaluating Student Speeches in Fundamentals of Speech" in this workbook as you answer this question.

Peer Evaluation Form for Round II—Speech to Inform

Speaker:_____ Date:_____

Topic: _____ Time:_____Critiquer: _____

Rating Scale: Excellent   Good   Average   Fair   Poor

                            5   4   3   2   1

Introduction: ____
  Gains attention
  Reveals the topic clearly
  Relates topic to the audience
  Establishes credibility
  Previews the body of the speech

Comments:_____

_____

Body: List the main points of the speech. On the line at right, note the kinds of supporting materials the speaker uses for each: (S) statistics; (E) examples; (T) testimonials.

Main Point   Supporting Materials

I._____   _____

II._____   _____

III._____   _____

Do the citations include the following information: who, where, and when?

      Citation #1_____

      Citation #2_____

      Citation #3_____

What pattern of organization does the speaker use for the body of the speech? (topical, chronological, or causal order)_____

                                           Excellent   Good   Average   Fair   Poor

                                                5   4   3   2   1

Conclusion: ____
  Reinforces the central idea
  Ends on a strong note

	Excellent 5	Good 4	Average 3	Fair 2	Poor 1
Delivery: ____					
Speaker's language clear					
Speaker's language appropriate					
Speaker maintains strong eye contact					
Speaker articulates words clearly					
Speaker seems poised and confident					
Speaker communicates enthusiasm					

Overall evaluation of speech:_____

_____

Peer Evaluation Form for Round II—Speech to Inform

Speaker:_____ Date:_____

Topic: _____ Time:_____ Critiquer: _____

Rating Scale:	Excellent	Good	Average	Fair	Poor
	5	4	3	2	1

Introduction: _____
  Gains attention
  Reveals the topic clearly
  Relates topic to the audience
  Establishes credibility
  Previews the body of the speech
Comments:_____

_____

Body: List the main points of the speech. On the line at right, note the kinds of supporting materials the speaker uses for each: (S) statistics; (E) examples; (T) testimonials.

Main Point   Supporting Materials

I._____   _____

II._____   _____

III._____   _____

Do the citations include the following information: who, where, and when?

     Citation #1_____

     Citation #2_____

     Citation #3_____

What pattern of organization does the speaker use for the body of the speech? (topical, chronological, or causal order)_____

	Excellent	Good	Average	Fair	Poor
	5	4	3	2	1

Conclusion: _____
  Reinforces the central idea
  Ends on a strong note

	Excellent 5	Good 4	Average 3	Fair 2	Poor 1

Delivery: ____
  Speaker's language clear
  Speaker's language appropriate
  Speaker maintains strong eye contact
  Speaker articulates words clearly
  Speaker seems poised and confident
  Speaker communicates enthusiasm

Overall evaluation of speech:_____

_____

Peer Evaluation Form for Round II—Speech to Inform

Speaker:_____ Date:_____

Topic: _____ Time:_____Critiquer: _____

Rating Scale:	Excellent	Good	Average	Fair	Poor
	5	4	3	2	1

Introduction: ____
  Gains attention
  Reveals the topic clearly
  Relates topic to the audience
  Establishes credibility
  Previews the body of the speech
Comments:_____

_____

Body: List the main points of the speech. On the line at right, note the kinds of supporting materials the speaker uses for each: (S) statistics; (E) examples; (T) testimonials.
Main Point   Supporting Materials

I._____   _____

II._____   _____

III._____   _____

Do the citations include the following information: who, where, and when?

  Citation #1_____

  Citation #2_____

  Citation #3_____

What pattern of organization does the speaker use for the body of the speech? (topical, chronological, or causal order)_____

	Excellent	Good	Average	Fair	Poor
	5	4	3	2	1

Conclusion: ____
  Reinforces the central idea
  Ends on a strong note

69

	Excellent 5	Good 4	Average 3	Fair 2	Poor 1

Delivery: ____
  Speaker's language clear
  Speaker's language appropriate
  Speaker maintains strong eye contact
  Speaker articulates words clearly
  Speaker seems poised and confident
  Speaker communicates enthusiasm

Overall evaluation of speech:_____

_____

Work Sheet for Identifying Parts and Types of Arguments for Round III—Speech to Persuade

Each of the six arguments written below fits best into one of the following argument types: example, analogy, causation, sign, definition, authority. Each type is represented in this exercise. To determine which argument represents which type, you must analyze the argument. Take it apart and identify its parts. The data of the argument represent the evidence. The claim is the conclusion to be drawn from the evidence. The type of argument on display can be ascertained by identifying the relationship between the data and the claim. To that end, begin by identifying the data and underlining once all words which represent DATA. Next, underline all words two times which represent CLAIM. In the spaces provided, write the WARRANT and TYPE OF ARGUMENT.

"Eighteen-year-olds can join the armed services to defend their country and walk into a voting booth to choose legislators because they are adults. Adults of this age should also be able to have a beer or any other type of alcoholic beverage if they choose."

Warrant_____

_____

Type of Argument_____

"This candidate for president of student government at Keene State College was president of her senior class in high school and did a great job. The positions are very similar. Let's vote for her so she can do a great job for us, too."

Warrant_____

_____

Type of Argument_____

"Professional basketball players earn too much money. Just look at the multi-million dollar contracts of several players, including O'Neal, Iverson, and Houston."

Warrant_____

_____

Type of Argument_____

"British scientists completed a study recently that concludes that 50 percent of smokers will die prematurely. Cigarettes are the cause of life-threatening illnesses."

Warrant_____

_____

Type of Argument_____

"The Wild Blueberry Association of North America predicts a low yield of wild blueberries in July and August, because of the lack of rain and the colder-than-usual temperatures in May and June."

Warrant_____

_____

Type of Argument_____

"Dr. Arthur Agatston, cardiologist and creator of the South Beach Diet, says his diet is a way of life, not a fad."

Warrant_____

_____

Type of Argument_____

Work Sheet for Preparing the Proposition

For each of the speeches to inform, you were required to write a thesis statement. For the speech to persuade you are required to write a proposition. The proposition is the conclusion you will advance, which will be backed up with evidence.

As you prepare the proposition for your speech to persuade, you will choose among three types: (1) the proposition of fact, (2) the proposition of value, or (3) the proposition of policy.

1. **Proposition of Fact**: A statement that reports, describes, predicts, or makes a causal claim. "Tanning beds cause skin cancer" is an example of a proposition of fact, because a causal claim is being made. Your audience will decide if the proposition is true or false on the basis of the evidence you supply.

2. **Proposition of Value**: A statement that presents a judgment about morality, beauty, merit, or wisdom. "Larry Bird is the greatest basketball player of all time" and "'The Swan' is a terrible television show" are examples of propositions of value. You may draw comparisons as well in this type of proposition. If you were to state, "Small colleges provide a better post-secondary experience than large universities," you would be presenting a proposition of value. Your audience will agree or disagree with your assessment once you have explained the criteria, justified those criteria, and connected the criteria of judgment to that which you would have them judge.

3. **Proposition of Policy**: A statement that urges that an action be taken or discontinued. "Social Security should be privatized" and "The Draft should be reinstituted" are examples of propositions of policy. Your audience will decide if they agree or disagree with your position. If they were to agree, they would be in favor of change. If the audience were to disagree, they would be in favor of maintaining the status quo.

Write the proposition for your speech to persuade. _____

_____

_____

Which type of proposition is it, and why? _____

_____

75

Work Sheet for Preparing the Practice Speech to Persuade Prior to Round III

Group's Assignment: Prepare a speech of five to eight (5-8) minutes to persuade with the use of visual aids. Because you will be completing the assignment during class time, the speech will be a work in progress. The assignment is designed to help you to use your textbook as a resource while selecting a topic, and researching and organizing a speech. Before you begin preparing the speech, select a group member who will act as the spokesperson for your group when your group is called upon to share your efforts with the class.

Planning Phase
Topic:

Proposition and its type (policy, value, or fact):

Method of Organization (problem/solution or logical reasons):

Reasons (data and claim) and their type (analogy, example, authority, causation, sign, definition)
    Data/Evidence and Claim/Conclusion   Type
1.

2.

3.

Presentation
Introduction:

Transition:

Body:
I.
    A.
        1.
        2.
    B.
        1.
        2.

Transition:

II.
    A.
        1.
        2.

B.
    1.
    2.

Transition:

III.
  A.
    1.
    2.
  B.
    1.
    2.

Transition:

Conclusion:
(Answer the following question: What do you want your audience to do to show you they have been convinced by your arguments?)

Work Sheet for Preparing Typed Outline for Round III—Speech to Persuade

Assignment: Prepare a speech of five to eight (5-8) minutes to persuade with the use of visual aids. You must cite three (3) sources in the body of the speech and include a bibliography (typed) of five (5) sources with your typed outline. Citations must include the following information: who is writing (or speaking), when the information was collected or reported, and where the information appears.

Sources to consider include full-length works, magazine articles, journal articles, newspaper articles, and televised documentaries. Interviews with experts in your topic area may also be used as source material. You must include photocopies of the first page of three (3) of your five (5) sources with your typed outline and bibliography, which is due the class day before you deliver your speech. Use complete sentences in the outline.

Due Date:_____

Planning Phase
Topic:

Proposition and its type (policy, value, or fact):

Method of Organization (logical reasons or problem/solution):

Reasons (data and claim) and their type (analogy, example, authority, causation, sign, definition)
      Data/Evidence and Claim/Conclusion   Type
1.

2.

3.

Presentation
Introduction:

Transition:

Body:

I.
    A.

        1.

        2.

B.
>   1.
>   2.

Citation:

Transition:

II.

A.
>   1.
>   2.

B.
>   1.
>   2.

Citation:

Transition:

III.

A.
>   1.
>   2.

B.
>   1.
>   2.

Citation:

Transition:

Conclusion:
(Answer the following question: What do you want your audience to do to show you they have been convinced by your arguments?)

Bibliography (use APA style):

If you choose the motivational pattern as a way to organize your speech, use the following outline format. Note: Two (2) citations are sufficient for a speech that utilizes this pattern of organization.

Planning Phase
Topic:

Proposition and its type (policy, value, or fact):

Reasons (data and claim) and their type (analogy, example, authority, causation, sign, definition)
    Data/Evidence and Claim/Conclusion   Type
1.

2.

3.

Presentation
Attention Step

A.

B.

Transition:

Need Step

A.

B.

Citation:

Transition:

Satisfaction Step

A.

B.

Citation:

Transition:

Visualization Step

A.

B.

Transition:

Action Step

A.

B.

Bibliography (use APA style):

Work Sheet for Preparing Introduction and Conclusion for Round III—Speech to Persuade

__Introduction__

The introduction is composed of two parts: the attention-getter and the preview. You have a variety of choices to make as you consider your opening: (1) startling statement, (2) rhetorical question, (3) story, (4) personal reference, (5) quotation, and (6) suspense. Refer to chapter 8 of your textbook for detailed explanations of each type. Then choose three (3) of the six (6) types and write three (3) possible attention-getters for your speech.

1. Startling Statement:

2. Rhetorical Question:

3. Story:

4. Personal Reference:

5. Quotation:

6. Suspense:

Conclusion

The conclusion is composed of two parts: the summary and the call to action. In a speech to persuade, you want to give your audience the opportunity to demonstrate that they have been convinced by your arguments. Write a plan of action for your speech.

Plan of Action:

Work Sheet for Preparing Key Word Outline for Round III
Speech to Persuade

All of your speeches for this course will be delivered extemporaneously, which means that each speech will be prepared, practiced, and delivered to an audience using a conversational tone and establishing nearly continuous eye contact. To that end, you will prepare detailed outlines during the preparation phase and key word outlines for use during the rehearsal stage and during the performance of the speech.

For the Speech to Persuade, you will use two 4"x 6" cards and turn them in to your instructor following your performance of the speech. Card #1: Write the Attention-Getter and the Statement of Emphasis in full. Use key words or short phrases that will remind you of your transitions and the main points of the Body of the speech. Insert indicators of the placement of the citations (C1, C2, C3). Card #2: Include the material you will cite--statistics, testimonials, and examples--and who is writing, where, and when.

Card #1:
Attention-Getter: Write in full.
Preview: Main points of the body of the speech.
Transition:
I.
C1
Transition:
II.
C2
Transition:
III.
C3
Transition:
Summary: Main points of the body of the speech.
Emphasis: Write in full.

Card #2:
Statistics, testimonials, and examples, with who is writing, where, and when.
Citation #1:

Citation #2:

Citation #3:

Instructor's Checklist for Typed Outline for Round III—Speech to Persuade

On the day you turn in your typed outline for this round of speeches, provide your instructor with this checklist. It will be used to grade your outline. Points: _____/80

Proposition (4)

_____Proposition is not included.

_____Proposition is not a statement of fact, policy, or value.

_____Proposition is not labeled.

_____Proposition is incorrectly labeled.

Method of Organization (3)

_____Method of organization is not noted.

_____Method of organization is incorrectly noted.

Reasons (18):

_____Reasons are not listed.

_____Reasons are incorrectly labeled. ___#1 ___#2 ___#3

_____Data are not included. ___#1 ___#2 ___#3

_____Claim is not included. ___#1 ___#2 ___#3

Introduction (6):

_____Introduction is not included in the outline.

Transitions (8):

_____Transitions are not included in the outline. ___#1 ___#2 ___#3 ___#4

_____Transitions do not serve as signposts or bridges to the next section of the speech.
                                        ___#1 ___#2 ___#3 ___#4

Body (12):

_____Outline of the body of the speech is not sufficiently detailed.

_____Complete sentences are not used.

_____Complete sentences are not used throughout the outline.

_____Incorrect format is used.

Citations (9):

_____Citations are not included in the outline. ___#1 ___#2 ___#3

_____Citations are incomplete. ___#1 ___#2 ___#3

Conclusion (6):

_____Action plan is not included.

Bibliography (14):

_____Five (5) sources are not included.

_____Incorrect format is used.

_____Photocopy of first page of three (3) of five (5) sources is not included.

Instructor's Evaluation Form for Round III—Speech to Persuade

Before you go to the front of the classroom to deliver your speech, provide your instructor with this form. It will be used to grade your performance.

Speaker:_____ Date:_____

Time: _____

Rating Scale:	Excellent	Good	Average	Fair	Poor
	5	4	3	2	1

INTRODUCTION:____
  Gains attention
  Reveals the topic clearly
  Relates topic to the audience
  Establishes credibility
  Previews the body of the speech
Comments:_____

_____

BODY: ____
  Arguments clear
  Arguments fully supported
  Sources credible
  Citations complete
  Organization well planned
  Emotional appeal effective
  Language accurate
  Language clear
  Language appropriate
  Transitions effective

Comments:_____

_____

CONCLUSION: ____
  Prepares audience for ending
  Reinforces the central idea
  Includes action plan
  Ends on a strong note
Comments:_____

_____

DELIVERY: ____
   Begins without rushing
   Maintains strong eye contact
   Avoids distracting mannerisms
   Articulates words clearly
   Uses pauses effectively
   Uses vocal variety to add impact
   Communicates enthusiasm
   Presents visual aids well
   Departs from the lectern without rushing
Comments:_____

_____

OVERALL EVALUATION____
Comments:_____

_____

_____

Maximum Points: 220   Points for Speech:_____/140 + Outline:_____/80

Total Points for Round:_____   Letter Grade:_____

Speech /140	Speech + Outline /220
A = 133	A = 209-220
AB = 126	AB = 198-208
B = 119	B = 187-197
BC = 112	BC = 176-186
C = 105	C = 165-175
CD = 98	CD = 154-164
D = 91	D = 143-153
F = Below 84	F = Below 132

Self-Evaluation of Performance of Speech to Persuade—Round III

Name_____ Date_____

Due: Class day after you perform your speech. Please record your responses to the questions in pen.

What were the best aspects of your speech? Give specific examples.
Organization:
  Method:

  Proportion:

Wording:

Delivery:

What, if anything, would you like to change about your speech?
Planning:

Organization:
  Method:

  Proportion:

Wording:

Delivery:

Estimate the number of hours you spent selecting your topic, researching the topic, and organizing the speech. Selecting topic_____ Researching speech_____ Organizing speech_____

Estimate the number of hours you spent rehearsing the speech. _____
What strategies did you use as you rehearsed the speech (rehearsed in front of friends, rehearsed in front of a mirror, rehearsed with a timer, rehearsed with a key word outline)?

How would you characterize your performance of this speech (outstanding, good, average, below average or poor) and why? Refer to the sheet called "Criteria Used for Evaluating Student Speeches in Fundamentals of Speech" in this workbook as you answer this question. In addition, include a brief discussion of the way you responded to the question(s) of your peers.

What are your strengths and weaknesses as a public speaker?

Peer Evaluation Form for Round III—Speech to Persuade

Speaker:_____ Date:_____

Topic: _____ Time:_____Critiquer: _____

Rating Scale:	Excellent	Good	Average	Fair	Poor
	5	4	3	2	1

Introduction: ____
  Gains attention
  Reveals the topic clearly
  Relates topic to the audience
  Establishes credibility
  Previews the body of the speech
Comments:_____

_____

Body: List the main points of the speech. On the line at right, note the kinds of arguments used to support the case (analogy, sign, causation, example, authority, or definition).

I._____   _____

II._____   _____

III._____   _____

Did the citations include the following information: who, where, and when?

    Citation #1_____

    Citation #2_____

    Citation #3_____

What pattern of organization did the speaker use for the body of the speech? _____
(Logical reasons, problem/solution, or motivational pattern)

Rating Scale:	Excellent	Good	Average	Fair	Poor
	5	4	3	2	1

Conclusion: ____
  Reinforces the central idea
  Ends on a strong note
What strategy did the speaker use for the action plan? _____
                                (cost/reward ratios or basic needs)

	Excellent 5	Good 4	Average 3	Fair 2	Poor 1
Delivery: ____					
Speaker's language clear					
Speaker's language appropriate					
Speaker maintains strong eye contact					
Speaker articulates words clearly					
Speaker seems poised and confident					
Speaker communicates enthusiasm					

Overall evaluation of speech_____

_____

Peer Evaluation Form for Round III—Speech to Persuade

Speaker:_____ Date:_____

Topic: _____ Time:_____Critiquer: _____

Rating Scale:	Excellent	Good	Average	Fair	Poor
	5	4	3	2	1

Introduction: ____
  Gains attention
  Reveals the topic clearly
  Relates topic to the audience
  Establishes credibility
  Previews the body of the speech
Comments:_____

_____

Body: List the main points of the speech. On the line at right, note the kinds of arguments used to support the case (analogy, sign, causation, example, authority, or definition).

I._____   _____

II._____   _____

III._____   _____

Did the citations include the following information: who, where, and when?

  Citation #1_____

  Citation #2_____

  Citation #3_____

What pattern of organization did the speaker use for the body of the speech? _____
(Logical reasons, problem/solution, or motivational pattern)

Rating Scale:	Excellent	Good	Average	Fair	Poor
	5	4	3	2	1

Conclusion: ____
  Reinforces the central idea
  Ends on a strong note
What strategy did the speaker use for the action plan? _____
                                        (cost/reward ratios or basic needs)

	Excellent	Good	Average	Fair	Poor
	5	4	3	2	1

Delivery: ____
   Speaker's language clear
   Speaker's language appropriate
   Speaker maintains strong eye contact
   Speaker articulates words clearly
   Speaker seems poised and confident
   Speaker communicates enthusiasm

Overall evaluation of speech_____

_____

Peer Evaluation Form for Round III—Speech to Persuade

Speaker:_____ Date:_____

Topic: _____ Time:_____Critiquer: _____

Rating Scale: Excellent   Good   Average   Fair   Poor
                         5   4   3   2   1

Introduction: ____
  Gains attention
  Reveals the topic clearly
  Relates topic to the audience
  Establishes credibility
  Previews the body of the speech
Comments:_____

_____

Body: List the main points of the speech. On the line at right, note the kinds of arguments used to support the case (analogy, sign, causation, example, authority, or definition).

I._____   _____

II._____   _____

III._____   _____

Did the citations include the following information: who, where, and when?

    Citation #1_____

    Citation #2_____

    Citation #3_____

What pattern of organization did the speaker use for the body of the speech? _____
(Logical reasons, problem/solution, or motivational pattern)

Rating Scale: Excellent   Good   Average   Fair   Poor
                         5   4   3   2   1

Conclusion: ____
  Reinforces the central idea
  Ends on a strong note
What strategy did the speaker use for the action plan? _____
                           (cost/reward ratios or basic needs)

	Excellent	Good	Average	Fair	Poor
	5	4	3	2	1

Delivery: ____

  Speaker's language clear

  Speaker's language appropriate

  Speaker maintains strong eye contact

  Speaker articulates words clearly

  Speaker seems poised and confident

  Speaker communicates enthusiasm

Overall evaluation of speech _____

_____

Critique Form for Final Examination

Name_____ Date_____

If your final examination includes critiquing a speech, bring this form with you to the final examination.

Instructions: From the notes that you write on this form after viewing the taped speech, organize and complete a critique that includes a discussion of the speaker, the message, and the audience.

Name of the speaker you observed_____

Event_____

Place of presentation_____

Distinguishing features of place, if any_____

_____

Topic of presentation _____

Type of speech (impromptu, extemporaneous, manuscript)_____

Checklist   **Comments**
Introduction
_____gained attention and interest_____

_____introduced topic clearly_____

_____related topic to audience_____

_____established credibility_____

_____previewed body of speech_____

Body
_____main points clear_____

_____main points fully supported_____

_____organization well planned_____

_____language accurate_____

_____language appropriate_____

_____transitions effective_____

Conclusion
_____prepared audience for ending_____

_____reinforced central idea_____

_____vivid ending_____

Delivery
_____began speech without rushing_____

_____maintained strong eye contact_____

_____avoided distracting mannerisms_____

_____articulated words clearly_____

_____used pauses effectively_____

_____used vocal variety to add impact_____

_____communicated enthusiasm for topic_____

_____departed from lectern without rushing_____

Overall Evaluation
_____specific purpose well chosen_____

_____message adapted to audience_____

_____held interest of audience_____

Student Evaluation of the *Fundamentals of Speech* Workbook

Please complete the evaluation and return to your instructor.

Semester _____ Section Number_____ Name(Optional)_____

Rating Scale: Circle the appropriate number.

1. The work sheets helped me with the preparation of the speeches.

5	4	3	2	1
Strongly Agree	Agree	Neutral	Disagree	Strongly Disagree

Comments:

2. The instructor's evaluation sheets adequately explained the goals of the assignments.

5	4	3	2	1
Strongly Agree	Agree	Neutral	Disagree	Strongly Disagree

Comments:

3. The peer critique forms helped me to plan my remarks when I was called upon to do so.

5	4	3	2	1
Strongly Agree	Agree	Neutral	Disagree	Strongly Disagree

Comments:

4. I would add the following items to the workbook:

5. I would remove the following items from the workbook: